ROMFORD

The heart of old Romford – the Golden Lion crossroads, *c.* 1905. The building housing the milliner's shop was later rebuilt to widen the entrance to North Street. The 'Lion' is mentioned in the will of Roger Reede in 1482 but it dates from before the creation of the Liberty of Havering in the Middle Ages.

BRITAIN IN OLD PHOTOGRAPHS

ROMFORD

BRIAN EVANS

SUTTON PUBLISHING LIMITED

Sutton Publishing Limited
Phoenix Mill · Thrupp · Stroud
Gloucestershire · GL5 2BU

First published 1998

Half title page photograph: Edward IV's granting
of a charter to the Liberty of Havering in 1486
helped to bring prosperity to the inhabitants of
the Romford area. From a commemorative
medallion designed by Ponthon; *title page
photograph*: the Laurie Hall at the
east end of the Market Place, first decade of
the twentieth century.

British Library Cataloguing in Publication Data
A catalogue record for this book is available from the
British Library.

ISBN 0-7509-1811-X

Typeset in 10/12 Perpetua.
Typesetting and origination by
Sutton Publishing Limited.
Printed in Great Britain by
Ebenezer Baylis, Worcester.

ACKNOWLEDGEMENTS

I am grateful to the following people for their help: Mrs B.M. Collett, Vernon Hood,
Arthur Gilbert and Family, Brian Luck and Stan Madell.

A white cow with its calves in a hurdle enclosure form a centre of interest, while sheep await sale in the
pens beyond. The premises of Harrison Barber, the horse slaughterers, are through under the arch.

CONTENTS

The eastern end of the market. Various animals are in their pens, waiting either to be sold or taken home again. In the centre background, with a white lower storey, two tall doorways and two windows, is the older Pig in Pound pub building. There are still many people living in the Market Place.

Airview of Romford, 1930. The dark building at bottom centre is the old police station in South Street. Above it the Arcade, Romford's first covered shopping area, is being constructed. The white building to the east of this is the recently built Plaza Cinema.

INTRODUCTION

The approach to Romford by and from the east is impressive and beautiful. Main Road with its attractive tree-lined pavements sweeps towards the town. Its greenery, gentle curves and undulations remind us of the fields and hedges which once lined this highway from London to Essex. As we pass over Black's Bridge the vista is of a wide sheet of water, now a feature of Raphael Park, which once graced the extensive estate of Gidea Hall. This famous property was once occupied by a tutor of the young King Edward VI, and was owned by a Lord Mayor of London. The Queen Dowager of France, Marie de Médici (the unpopular mother of Queen Henrietta Maria) came to Gidea Hall in 1638, and Sir Anthony Cooke entertained Elizabeth I at his splendidly rebuilt version of the hall, which he had recently completed, in 1568. Apart from the lake in the park there also remain two smaller ornamental ponds, once part of the great estate and now adorning the back gardens of houses on the Gidea Park Garden Suburb.

In this book we recapture the life of the famous market town before and after 1900 and also recall the history of the two hamlets of Squirrels Heath and Hare Street, which lie a short way to the east but have now been subsumed into the greater area of Gidea Park and Heath Park. The pace of life before 1930 was slower and gentler, the home was more important and small pleasures such as visits to other members of the family or a half day's outing by bicycle into the countryside were common because there were few cars and little money for luxuries.

In the not too distant past Romford was of interest to visitor and native alike. The cattle being driven to and from, or being auctioned at, the market was a great free entertainment, as were the performances put on by the 'characters' who traded from the stalls. Television had not been invented but the show put on by the spielers to sell their goods quickly, often starting with bargains or giveaways in order to lure the watchers into a purchase, was a worthy forerunner of the television game show.

There were many other characters – shopkeepers, police, delivery staff – in the days when Romford was full of surprises, but the individuality of the town did not depend just on these people, it was also the built environment which set Romford apart. How many places in Britain had such an odd-shaped building as the Laurie Hall, which in its prime served a multitude of purposes except the one for which it was built? How many towns could boast an ancient court house still standing into the 1930s? The court house in Romford, located at the South Street end of the Market Place, survived until 1933 and it was here that the venerable old Liberty of Havering had dispensed its own local justice with none in authority above it but the monarchy. In fact Romford was full of old architecture which by its very age had gathered stories and legends. Roger Reede's almshouses continued a 500-year-old tradition on a site in North Street till the end of the 1960s, and the Charity School of 1728 with its later additions remained in use as a library before being demolished about the same time. Of these great treasures, sadly only a few vestiges survive. The almshouses and school continue in new buildings, but the old could have been put to some new use – retaining some of the specialness of Romford. We have retained Church House, the oldest domestic building in the town itself, which for centuries was in fact an inn. We still have the Golden Lion at the very centre of Romford's history, dating back well over 500 years and connected with the writer and philosopher Sir Francis Bacon. One of the oldest railway heritage buildings in the world at Squirrels Heath has recently received preservation status. In this collection of photographs there is another unique structure reminding us of the forerunners of the National Health Service – the Old Workhouse at Oldchurch Hospital whose importance has been undervalued. No other surviving example of the earliest Victorian workhouses has such character as this one with several original features intact. Under threat with the anticipated relocation of the hospital to an adjacent site, it would be to the everlasting shame of the town if it did not survive as an integral part of any new development. One potential use could be as a museum displaying Romford's splendid medical heritage.

Because of the existence of so many old buildings Romford to many of its visitors in the earlier years of the twentieth century must have seemed ageless. Even then the cattle market was nearly 700 years old and on Wednesdays it reigned supreme, gathering in customers and traders from many miles around. The nucleus of the town – the Market Place, High Street, North Street and South Street – was still quite small. A great sea of countryside existed around its edges where the town abruptly finished. The area had a unique and ancient history with Royal connections.

Yet the town was already changing, imperceptibly for a few years, but then with real momentum. Photographers captured the beginning of this process, including the loss of the town's quaint architecture and with it some of Romford's special character. In this book we can enjoy both its former glories and the advance of the modern age in Romford and in the hamlets of Hare Street and Squirrels Heath to the east.

CHAPTER ONE

SURROUNDED BY HISTORY

On both sides of the Market Place there were alleyways and arched entrances into courts and yards – a hidden Romford. This is Smith's Yard by artist Alfred Bennett Bamford, a native Romfordian who explored its byways at the end of the nineteenth century. After becoming an art teacher he found time to wander into and record interesting corners that have gradually disappeared. We owe a great debt to Bamford for making us aware of the rich architectural heritage of Romford. It was often the back view of a structure that revealed its true age, as Bamford well understood – the front and more public side had often been refaced to keep up with the latest fashion.

Church House, seen here in the 1930s, is the oldest domestic building in the town. Constructed in the 1400s it has deceptive charm and stands on the spot by the church where Romford began. In 1406 a piece of woodland here was cut down for the building of a new church, marking the flight of citizens from the frequently flooded town at Oldchurch and the birth of a new community. In 1486, after use as a private dwelling, the building seen here became a chantry house for the priest under the terms of Avery Cornburgh's will. The priest was to go daily into the church and say prayers for the immortal souls of the Cornburgh household. After chantries were done away with by Henry VIII it spent centuries as an inn, at first the Chequers and later the Cock and Bell until it closed in the early years of the twentieth century.

Opposite. This Georgian style town house, 33 Market Place, was built on the site of the house/apothecary's shop where the notorious Colonel Blood sought refuge for his wife and family, disguised under the name of Weston, in 1668. It was from here that he set out to rescue his friend Capt Mason, who was being taken under armed guard to the northern assizes for trial. He succeeded in liberating his friend but was wounded five times and had to make his way back as best he could to Romford. Here he lay low until his wounds healed. He later planned the daring robbery of the Crown Jewels from the Tower of London, but mysteriously was eventually pardoned and given a pension by Charles II.

Roger Reede founded his almshouses in the fifteenth century on the west side of North Street, and there they remained for 500 years until the end of the 1960s when preparations for the new Romford ring road meant their demolition and rebuilding in Church Lane. The site now lies under the roundabout and pedestrian underpass at the entrance to St Edward's Way and the junction with North Street.

North Street in 1906, full of timber and tile buildings, many the homes of tradesmen and craftsmen. The Express Office of a local newspaper on the right has been housed in the original Congregational chapel, built in 1823 and replaced by the one in South Street in 1877.

Marshalls House, in its wooded setting by an attractive lake. This Georgian house, demolished in 1960, stood on a site which had been occupied by a succession of mansions as far back as an estate recorded in 1213. Like many Essex houses it derives its name from an ancient owner – one William Marescall was a witness to a local document dated 1189. These names have come down through the centuries and are now written without the apostrophe that originally signified 'the house of'.

Marshalls Park, 1925. The rather confused style of the architecture is partly visible through the climbing vegetation, once so fashionable.

Gidea Hall, 1914. It is seen from the meadow on the south side, which today is occupied by the Gidea Park Lawn Tennis Club courts. The turret on the stable block is clearly visible. The second Gidea Hall was built in about 1720, but older parts of the house remained.

The old court yard at Gidea Hall, *c.* 1910. Apparently a survivor of a previous house, this group of buildings harks back to Tudor England and may have been the remains of the building dating in part back to 1467. It formed a wonderful backdrop to a pageant of Romford's history held here before the First World War. By 1802 the estate had extended to 620 acres.

The crowd passing Laurie Square are progressing up Main Road towards the gates of the new Raphael Park for the official ceremony of presentation to the town, 2 June 1904. The park had been created out of the westernmost section of the old Gidea Hall estate. Herbert Raphael, who was to become an MP and was later knighted, donated it. He had already laid out Romford Golf Course on the eastern portion and would soon develop the remaining part as the Gidea Park Garden Suburb.

Raphael Park preserved within its boundaries a pleasant and sizeable portion of woodland, open space and lake, retaining for public use a section of the countryside fast disappearing from Romford's outskirts.

The beautiful Black's Bridge, seen to best advantage from within the park, was part of the eighteenth-century improvements to Gidea Hall. The bridge of three elliptic arches was designed by James Wyatt. It is built of red brick in a mixture of English and header bond with stucco piers to the central arch and a Portland stone coping.

The ancient gabled house of different centuries which once graced Romford High Street are seen here in about 1905.

Children in their Sunday best watch the camera at the west end of Romford High Street, 1906. In the centre left is the Jubilee Coffee Tavern, providing a touch of Victorian culture – and an attempt to create a teetotal oasis in a neighbourhood dedicated to alcohol.

The hamlet of Hare Street at Romford's eastern perimeter, 1910. The White Hart Inn, until recently converted into the old cottages, has, remarkably for Romford, survived and is now again a place of refreshment, known as The Archers.

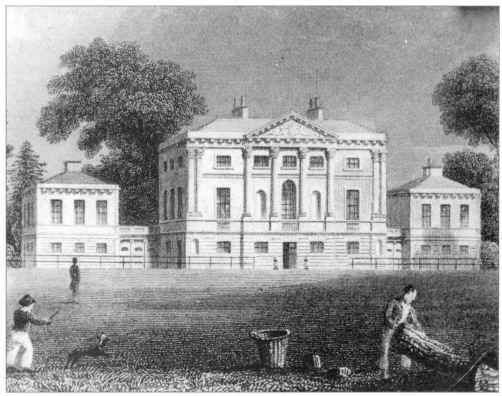

A detail of Hare Hall, *c.* 1830. This mansion, designed for J.A. Wallinger by James Paine, is a minor masterpiece. Built in 1768/9 and added to in the late nineteenth century, it is now part of the Royal Liberty School. It is hoped that sufficient funds can be raised to restore the structure and make it better known.

In 1916 the hall and grounds were taken over as an army training centre for First World War troops under the banner of the Artists' Rifles. It is to their credit that the house survived their occupation intact unlike many others. Part of the grounds were developed after the war and many of the roads bear the names of owners and others connected with the hall.

The Artists' Rifles, 2nd Battalion, band march through the huts erected on the meadows of the Hare Hall estate.

An imaginative impression of the house and grounds used as a cover design for the Royal Liberty School magazine. The school opened in the hall and remaining grounds in 1921 and subsequently newer school units were built.

The Pavement, at the top end of Romford Market Place stretching from Laurie Hall up to the site of the old turnpike and facing Laurie Square. The nearest (light-coloured) Georgian houses later acquired shopfronts.

Part of the Charity School group of buildings. The original building dated from 1728 although the school existed elsewhere since 1711. The main school bears a foundation plaque and niches with the figures of the Charity Boy and Girl and is flanked on the right by the later Schoolmaster's House, to the right of which (out of the picture) is a substantial extension block. This group remained until the end of the 1960s and the construction of Mercury Gardens as part of the ring road.

Collier's Mill House with the post mill and steam mill, seen in an early photograph using the wet plate process. These stood on the area of land now occupied by Hill Court, Main Road and were pulled down in about 1865.

The last days of an old building where the Toll Gate had once stood, above the Pavement. Redevelopment is taking place to build the Dolphin Leisure Centre in the 1980s.

The Cooke monument in St Edward's Church, Market Place, records one of the town's greatest families who lived at Gidea Hall. The photograph was taken in July 1973 before the monument was partially restored through the intervention of Charles Whitwood and the Romford and District Historical Society.

The Round House at Havering-Atte-Bower village. The official listing gives its date as about 1792, built for William Sheldon, but it may be earlier. Because of its oval shape it has been claimed that it was built in the shape of a classical tea caddy.

CHAPTER TWO

WHEN ALE WAS KING

The Duke of Wellington, one of numerous hostelries to have been banished from the face of Romford. The enormous quantity of alcohol consumed in past days was partly the result of a need to replace liquid lost during a hard day's labour. The public houses also provided essential places to exchange news, gossip and bargains, business or personal. They even provided rooms for legal, medical and educational offices. Rooms were often hired out to doctors, dentists, barbers and other useful professions. On market day many people from miles around came to town and most spent part of the day in a hostelry. Those that are now gone include The Queen's Arms, King's Arms, King's Head, Windmill and Bells, Drover's Arms, Pig in the Pound, Dolphin, Cock and Bell, Three Crowns and the White Swan. Many others have disappeared from other parts of the town such as the High Street, North Street, Waterloo Road and London Road. It is interesting to note that drinking places are now making a massive comeback, particularly to South Street – the wheel of history has turned full circle.

Ind Coope's brewery yard with its railway system stretching back from the brewery frontage in High Street, 1908.
Many of the workers at the brewery lived in the cottages on the former Barrack Ground estate in Waterloo Road,
which can be seen in the middle distance. On the left is the spire of St Andrew's Church, built with the help of

brewery money. Barrels are stacked high in the yard. Not a lorry is to be seen for these were the years of horse and cart delivery and the stables are to the right of the photograph. The whole of this site is now awaiting development, having been suddenly closed a few years short of its 200th anniversary.

The 40 acres of the brewery are viewed from a slightly different angle in this advertisement. The layout was complicated and subtle changes occurred all the time. The railway system that took wagons loaded with beer under the railway bank and through the sidings on to the main line for distribution is clearly shown. In the late nineteenth century there were 2 miles of track within the premises and 2 locomotives (Eclipse and Oscar) which brought in and took out upwards of 400 trucks daily.

The rebuilt White Hart is seen here in 1921 in its premises on the north-east side of the brewery, facing the High Street.

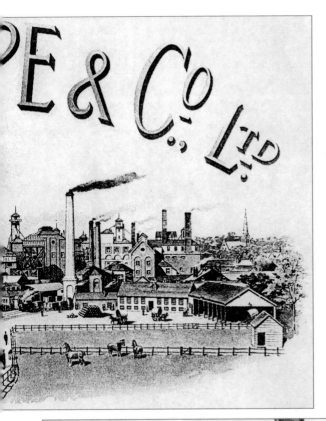

The inn yard of the ancient White Hart, which was recorded as early as 1489. The building here was demolished in 1896. The yard could accommodate several of the stage coaches that travelled the great Essex road between London and towns in East Anglia — the road through the High Street was then the chief route to the eastern counties of England.

An aerial view above the brewery in 1930 shows its importance to the economy and life of the
town. A significant part of the complex was the employee's sports ground. Social provision for the
families who worked there encouraged son to follow father in Ind Coope employment, and
pensioners were particularly well looked after. Outside the premises new features of Romford such

as the Romford Telephone Exchange, the tall white building to the right of the centre of the picture, and the South Street Arcade, the white building on the far right with a flat roof and next to the dark building of the old police station, can be picked out.

The Coach and Bell public house, opposite the brewery in Romford High Street, pictured before demolition. This inn is mentioned in a church register of 1683.

The Liberty Arms near the top end of Waterloo Road competed with the Romford Arms in the High Street for the title of smallest pub in Romford. The pub may have developed from the canteen used by the soldiers at the former barracks on the site during the Napoleonic threat.

The Sun in London Road, 1889. It had been on this site since at least 1632. When the Compasses, another pub next to it (out of the picture), moved to Abbs Cross, Hornchurch, the Sun was rebuilt on the vacant plot. The Sun's old site has become a car park.

The King's Head is mentioned in records of 1714 but the building shown here was much older. Like many of the former market inns it had an archway and yard for vehicles behind with attached stables. It was replaced by a Victorian building and latterly had a large function hall at the rear.

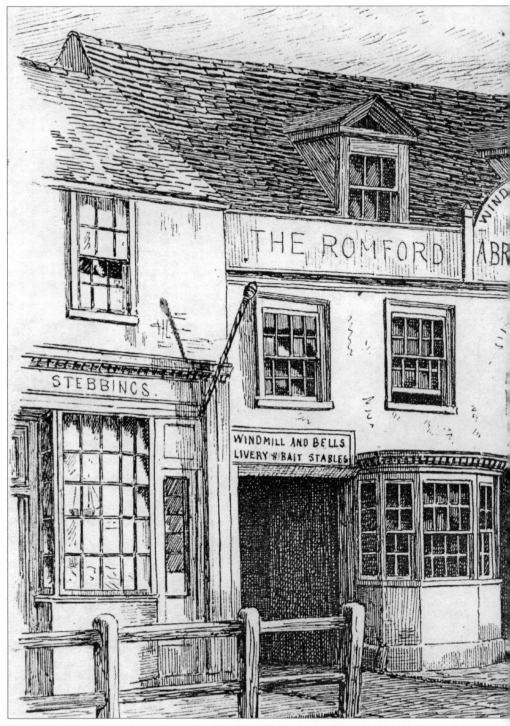

The Windmill and Bells, drawn by Bamford in 1889, looks very Dickensian. One could imagine the Wellers having one of their strange conversations in the ostler's yard. The inn is not mentioned in early church registers, which suggests that its name was changed, as the structure was clearly centuries old. Stone's drapery store on the right celebrated its centenary before becoming a branch

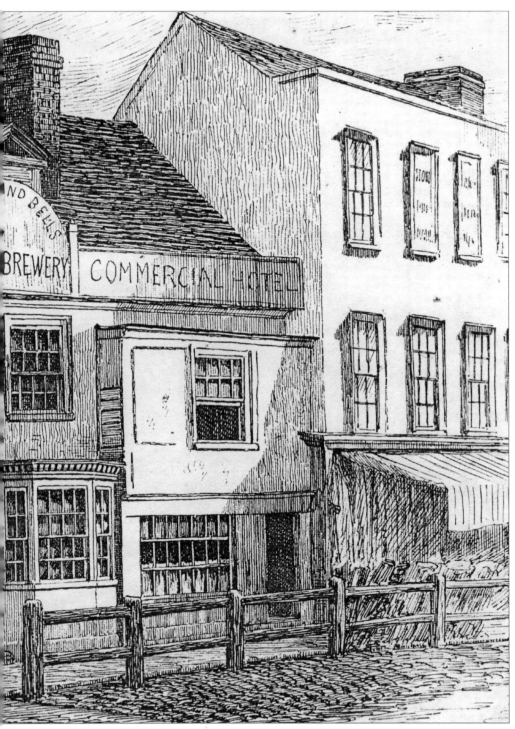

of Debenhams. Stebbings on the left displays the old style barber's pole and combined two quite different trades, being described as hairdresser *and* woodturner. Presumably the owner only managed to practise both with the help of assistants.

A side view of the White Swan building in the Market Place (this section was used as Attwood's grocer's shop), just before demolition in 1967. The site is now part of Swan Walk pedestrian passage. The inn could be traced back to at least 1468 and is pictured on the left of a famous early nineteenth-century engraving of Romford market bearing a large plaster figure of a swan above its frontage.

The Fox and Hounds at the top end of South Street, 1903. It was entered by means of two steps up and care needed to be exercised in coming away after an evening's drinking. This site is now under the roadway and widened pavement.

An Ind Coope drayman carrying an old wooden barrel and a crate of beer bottles is used to advertise the company's products, in this case from the Burton side of the business. The Edwardian era saw a boom in the heavy promotion of brands that we see today. This lithograph in colour was used as an insert in other publications and promoted three local off-licences in Romford.

Some hectic market trading is going on in front of the Swan Inn and Blucher's Head at the turn of the
century. At the beginning of the First World War the name of the latter pub was changed to the Duke of

Wellington to counter the strong feelings of the patriotic masses against all German-sounding names.
Squeezed in between the two is the old established family grocer, B. Wallis.

The entrance into North Street, 1930s. The block on the right, opposite the Golden Lion, had been rebuilt further back since Edwardian times in order to widen the roadway for traffic. The Golden Lion itself, dating back to the 1400s, came under threat in the 1950s to provide more room for the greedy motor vehicle. Luckily commonsense prevailed and it remained as a historical landmark, of which there are now so few in Romford.

The tranquil country scene that once reigned at what is now the busy hub of rail and bus interchange. The windmill could not operate after the great railway bank was built next to it in 1839, although it remained in situ for years. Whitmore's Steam Flourmills used the site, fronting on Victoria Road from about 1858 (see p. 124, top). The Rising Sun pub lived on in name in a new building, renamed in recent years as the Morland Arms.

The Coach and Bell in the High Street, *c.* 1890. It had extensive outbuildings at the rear. It suffered several times from flooding by the River Rom, for instance in August 1888.

The last days of the Swan Inn, Romford Market Place. The photograph was taken on a summer Sunday in 1966.

A revealing glimpse of old Romford High Street, 1920s. Tucked in among a large number of small shops on the left is The Romford Arms, soon to go out of business. After it was closed it is said to have been used as a

greengrocer's. The High Street was chiefly famous for its speciality butchers', many of them long established such as Poston's and Axon's.

London Road, 1920s. On the extreme left of the photograph is seen the west end of the New Mill Inn which stood on the old corner of Waterloo Road. This corner was removed to create the ring road, roundabout and pedestrian underpass under which the site now lies. Edwin Light was the landlord in 1905 and by 1910 J.E. Yull was installed.

The Star Inn next to Romford station, 1919. It was named after the original Star which is purported to have been in the High Street and which was the original brewhouse that started Romford Brewery. With the railway next door, a busy horse and later motor cab service operated from the open space between. The widening of the railway in 1930 consumed this open area.

The rebuilt Crown Hotel in London Road, 1920. Once a country pub on the outskirts of the town, business was to flourish with the opening of Romford Greyhound Stadium opposite.

Long gone are the King's Arms and the premises of G. Steel, boot, shoe and leather seller, next door, located in what were apparently sixteenth-century premises. Bamford drew this in 1880.

These were the days when Romfordians could lean over the bridge in Romford High Street and look at the River Rom flowing beneath. In this 1920s view the Rom bridge is on the far left while opposite are B. Grant's van and store, which traded in wines and spirits and formed part of the brewery frontage. Many small businesses flourished opposite the brewery at this time, when Arthur Daer was landlord of the Golden Lion: Pink's, Meadmore's (restaurant), Fletcher's (newsagent), Pearsons' (watchmaker and jeweller), Tidmarsh's (baker/confectioner), Dexter's & Blackwell's (butchers), and Masel's (household goods).

CHAPTER THREE

SQUIRRELS HEATH & HARE STREET

A peaceful, rural scene at Squirrels Heath, 1906. The tiny church of All Saints is seen beyond the sign of The Squirrel's Head on the right. The name almost certainly derives from a family who are mentioned in thirteenth-century documents as Scurell and Esquirell. Brentwood Road had only a few houses at this time. The opening of the Great Eastern Railway factory to the east of the Brentwood Road bridge in the middle of the nineteenth century brought an initially slow population growth. Many of the workers were housed in Factory Road just to the south and there was even a school in two converted cottages. For many years the nearest stations were Romford and after 1868 Harold Wood. Gidea Park station was not built until late 1910 to serve the new Gidea Park Garden Suburb, built mainly north of Hare Street.

You can almost hear the birds singing as you look at this peaceful country lane with its surrounding fields that was Squirrels Heath in 1916.

The buildings in this photograph of Hare Hall Lane (Brentwood Road) in 1904 are still there today, though there are slightly fewer trees and considerably more in the way of traffic. However, at least pedestrians now have the footpath to keep them safe.

Poole's Bakery at Squirrels Heath, 1908. The staff are seen in front of the substantial premises which were a landmark in the area for many years. The bakery was an important employer – deliveries were made to the growing number of small shops servicing the new houses being built or were taken round the streets in the bakery's own vehicles. A block of flats now occupies the site.

Dating back centuries, this old oak at the beginning of Manor Avenue was destroyed in the great storm of 1987. Might it once have been a 'moot' tree for local people to resolve disputes?

New features were appearing at the Squirrels Head crossroads by the 1920s: lamp posts, signposts and even a white line to guide vehicles around what could be a hazardous corner. The extension has been built on the side of All Saints and new houses are visible in Squirrels Heath Lane. A later change was to occur when a direct hit by a

parachute mine obliterated the church and hall on 10 May 1941; the public house was also damaged. The church was eventually rebuilt at Ardleigh Green at the far end of the lane.

Brentwood Road near the Drill Inn, Squirrels Heath, 1920s. There are some newer bungalows built on a plot between Victorian cottages. A road gang is either repairing the roadway or making up the rudimentary sidewalk. On the right-hand side is a hedgeline.

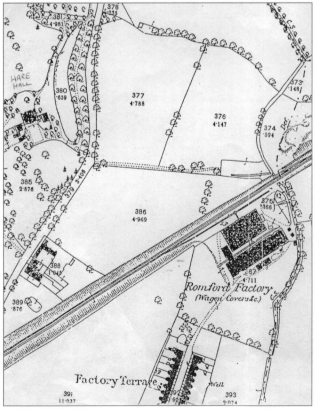

A map of the area around the Squirrels Heath railway factory, 1870. At this time there were still fields and hedgerows. The Great Eastern Railway had a constant need for tarpaulin covers for the thousands of open railway wagons used. Railways were then the major transporter and distributor of every kind of produce the length and breadth of Britain, road transport playing only a subsidiary role. The factory had started life as the locomotive works – a predecessor of Stratford.

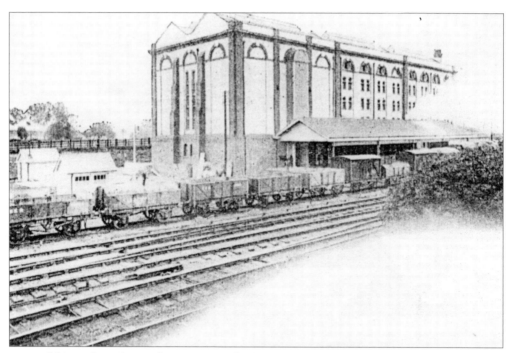

A second factory for making and mixing provender for the thousands of carthorses delivering goods at the end of their rail journey was built next to the old works and nearer Brentwood Road. This was later burnt down at the end of the 1960s. A modern store occupies the site.

The railway school was eventually replaced by a new one in Salisbury Road in 1911 on a 2 acre site. Attached but separate was a 'special' school. In this photograph a class of pupils at the main Elementary School are taking the photographer very seriously.

A glimpse of a garage forecourt in the golden age of motoring. Heath Park Garage was opened in 1928 by the brothers Arthur and Wyatt Gilbert and remarkably the business is still run by the same family today. This shows

the premises a year or so after its foundation, with Power petrol at 1*s* 3*d* a gallon. The garage soon gained a franchise for the once famous Singer cars.

Old cottages in Brentwood Road opposite the original Heath Park Garage premises demolished for further garage operations.

Extension to the original garage premises. Through mergers and takeovers the original Singer franchise became Rootes Group, then Chrysler, Talbot and is now Peugeot.

A little bleak in its position at the country crossroads, the Drill Inn in the 1920s was at least adjacent to a postbox and street light. Suburbia in the shape of Manor Avenue estate (behind the photographer) was making advances.

A more cheerful scene at the Drill Inn. Workmen are erecting ladders for a spring clean. The clearly visible signs, indicating the names of the exit roads from the crossing, are a pointer to an increase in traffic.

The Drill intersection, looking north-east, 1930. The triangle of land, part of the old heath, is now occupied by houses.
To the left the fenced plot awaits the construction of the present shopping parade (end of Heath Park Road).

Above, in the 1920s Balgores Lane contained houses that were built following the Gidea Park Garden Suburb development. In the lower picture more development has taken place by the 1930s, lining this important route between Romford and Hornchurch.

In 1900 Hare Street village was a pleasant country walk from Romford. The old style Essex weatherboard cottages are much closer to the highway than the present development line on the north side of the road, much of it no longer village dwellings. It is now almost entirely devoted to commerce and professional services. In this picture a local inhabitant looks over the fence on the left to see what traffic, if any, is on the road – horse-driven of course at this time. The empty plot on the right became a row of shops with flats above, built as part of the new Garden Suburb.

Hare Street under snow, 1902. Notice the Unicorn public house at the edge of the carriageway, later rebuilt to the north in its present position with a walkway in front.

A close-up of the old White Hart block, south of and facing the Unicorn and Ship. By 1914 this was no longer a public house but instead a place of light refreshment for cyclists, walkers and others. The hamlet was quite soon to be overrun with soldiers from the Artists' Rifles, whose camp was built (with an entrance a short way up the main road) across the fields of Hare Hall.

It is 1916 and the village of Hare Street is buzzing with activity on the arrival of the Artists Rifles. Huts had been constructed in the grounds of the Hare Hall estate and soldiers from the camp can be seen in the distance. Several

new businesses have sprung up in the village to serve the needs of the soldiers – cafés and tailoring shops among them.

Staff outside the Romford Golf Club, 1910. The club was formed after a meeting at the Golden Lion in February 1894 attended by prominent local men and including representatives of the Whitehall Golfers' Club. Shortly after it was opened, membership had grown to 200 men and more than 50 ladies, and according to *Golfing* magazine the clubhouse was 'fitted up in a style which should meet the requirements of the most fastidious'. There were four large bedrooms upstairs and 'a fine smoking room . . . which provides a cosy lounge', on the ground floor besides a luncheon room 'where excellent repasts are served'.

CHAPTER FOUR

ROMFORD PEOPLE

Mr Bassett acts as the marshal of the Romford Carnival, appropriately on horseback, 1929. The planning of floats and their decoration was an activity which lasted all year. At this time the procession would form in the Victoria Road area, some floats being prepared in the side streets, and the marshal would ride to and fro regulating the order of the procession. The floats finished up on Swan Field, where the Town Hall now stands. The object of the event was to raise money for the Victoria Cottage Hospital in Pettits Lane and Romfordians gave generously while enjoying a spectacle that appealed immensely in the days before television and all the competing attractions of the present day. The carnival contributed to the community spirit which was to serve the town so well in the Second World War.

Spectators, including mums pushing their children in old style prams, watch from the pavement of Victoria Road as the carnival gets under way, 1929. At this time shoppers could purchase all their needs from the establishments in this road without going further afield, although they would have to enter a large number of individual traders' premises to do so.

Romfordians all dressed up for the special day thoroughly enjoy the activities provided by the carnival organisers at the end of the 1929 procession.

Lining up for the start of the 1929 carnival.

A plane with a winged message at the same carnival.

1. GEORGE MEAD
2. RICHARD PARKER
3. JAMES PARKER
4. GEORGE TAVERNER
5. JOHN DAY
6. JOHN SMITH

The Romfo

This lithograph by J.C. Anderson of the Romford cricket team of 1850 is a remarkable social document, giving us an insight into the carefully structured society of the town at that time. As has been pointed out by J.R. Clube in *Romford Record No. 22* this was a time of transition in cricket. Top hats for players were on

8. RICHARD CARTER
9. ALFRED HARVEY
10. WILLIAM SPENCER
11. THOMAS BOURNE
12. JOSEPH HAMMOND
13. EDWARD KIMPTON
14. JOHN CLUBE
A. WARWICK

Cricket Club.

the way out and caps were becoming the accepted gear – two of the team sport them, one of them John Clube who was a hatter by trade. New spliced bats were coming in – the one in the middle of the picture, held by William Busby, is spliced.

This delightful Edwardian view of London Road, near the Salem chapel, shows cyclists enjoying the freedom of a traffic-free environment. At this time bicycles were used for many quite lengthy journeys as well as for shorter trips.

The Clarion Cycling Club at Romford. The location of the clubhouse is not known.

Another group photograph of the Clarion Club. Social clubs such as this facilitated the breakdown of the rigid social hierarchies of Victorian England. This dispelling of some of the taboos was later accelerated by the demands of the First World War when people from different classes began to work side by side. The small emancipations achieved were widened after the war as the 'swinging' twenties reaped the freedoms of a more enlightened age.

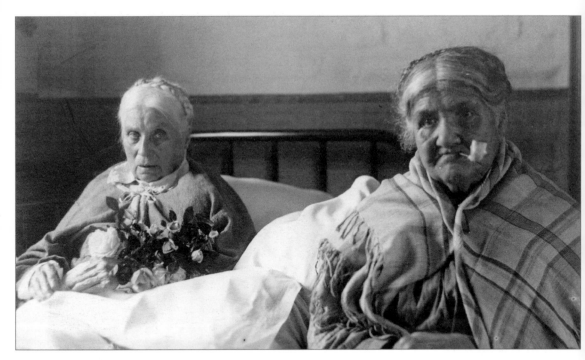

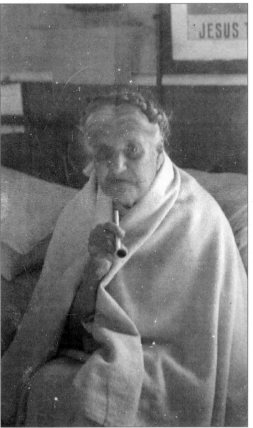

These remarkable ladies from Romford had both passed their centuries (actually 102) and had their photographs printed in a national newspaper. They were living at the Elizabethan house behind the south side of the Market Place known as the Retreat, although their exact circumstances are not known. To live to 100 was very unusual before the 1950s. However, the Romford area certainly excelled other places in the longevity stakes, as various records of the nineteenth century show.

The Zulus, a group of entertainers who raised funds for charity. Their 'scoreboard' seems to record prizes won in carnivals.

A 'family group' photograph of people connected with the Romford branch of the National Union of Railwaymen. Membership gave many benefits and assistance in times of trouble before the welfare state. The social and entertainment side of these organisations was important before the advent of large-scale public entertainment. An old railway coach is being used as a pavilion, so the location is probably the railway sports field below the station at Romford, now occupied by the cinema and Regarth Avenue.

BIRD'S NEST IN A LETTER-BOX.

MR. ALFRED SMEE, in his very interesting volume, entitled "Instinct and Reason," adduces many curious instances of birds selecting strange localities for their nesting-places; but we question whether either of his instances exceeds in singularity the specimen here Illustrated, from a sketch by Peter Bearblock, Esq., of Hornchurch.

The penny postage having greatly increased the bulk as well as the number of postal communications, the apertures through which the letters are put have been proportionally enlarged; and, in this case, it has facilitated a strange departure from general rule. Withinside the door of the Post-office at Squirrel's-Heath, near Hornchurch, a pair of those beautiful birds, the Blue Titmouse, having entered by the orifice made for the posting of letters, have contrived to carry therein an incredible mass of materials for nidification, as feathers, hair, and moss, covering the entire floor of the box some inches deep; in the centre of which they have made their little nursery, and are now rearing ten little ones. The hen kept her post, while sitting, three weeks, notwithstanding being daily covered up with letters and newspapers; as many as thirty of the former having been removed from around her on several occasions. With this interruption, besides letters and newspapers continually dropped into the box, the bird has built her nest, laid her eggs (each about the size of a pea), and carried on incubation; all the ten eggs have been

BLUE TITMOUSE'S NEST IN A LETTER-BOX NEAR HORNCHURCH.

hatched, and, at the date of our Correspondent's letter, this moderate family were expected to come out into the feathered world in a few days.

A page from a mid-nineteenth century magazine which refers to the post office at Squirrels Heath.

Visitors to Romford market, 24 June 1904. The stalls still sold mainly farming produce and items connected with agriculture. For clothes and household items and many other consumer goods now sold in the market one would have needed to visit the mostly small and locally owned shops dotted around the Market Place and in the High Street and parts of South Street and North Street.

Workers from a Squirrels Heath nursery garden setting out on a 'Beano' outing – a rare break in the working year – early in the twentieth century.

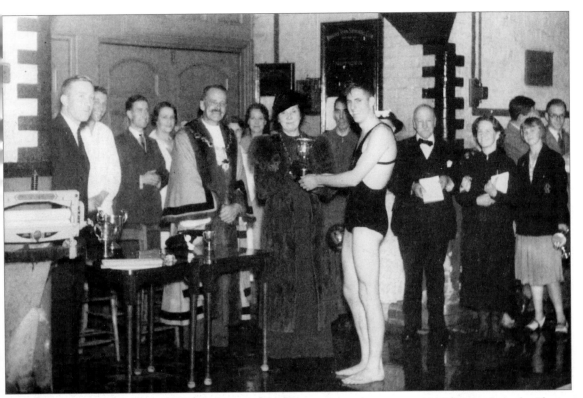

The winning swimmer at a gala held to celebrate Romford's new borough status receives his prize from the Charter Mayor, Charles H. Allen, 1937. The venue is Mawney Road baths, which were eventually demolished in 1975.

The short-lived Havering Court open-air pool at Chase Cross, packed with swimmers in the summer of 1937.

Mayor Blane attends the event of a lifetime – the official proclamation of Queen Elizabeth II's accession on 8 February 1952, outside the Town Hall.

A happy and joyous occasion – Fairford Way's street party to celebrate the Coronation, 1953.

A Coronation party for the children of Salisbury Road, 1953.

A festive group photographed at a special cricket match organised by the Romford & District Cricket League at the brewery sports ground in Coronation year, 1953.

This delightful view of the Barton Avenue Coronation tea recalls the lost innocent of the 1950s when childhood was more carefree and longer than it is today – the teenage revolution and youth culture would arrive in a few short years with the coming of the 1960s.

CHAPTER FIVE

LEGACY OF A CENTURY
(BEFORE 1914)

A train arriving at Romford station, 1904. The century before 1914 had been one of growth, progress and finally consolidation. Whole streets of houses had been built, one after the other, as Romford's population increased dramatically. The main line railway arrived in 1839 and must have seemed an anachronism to many in the country town of that time. However, the limited service on only one pair of tracks perched high above the town brought London and the rest of the country nearer, even though at first used only by a minority of locals. Local traders prospered, serving not only an increasing number of Romford residents but also the wider region not served by the railway. Romford became the centre of a range of facilities, social as well as business. Like many important places it raised a volunteer fire service. The Romford service was led by a very able person, Capt Sam Davis who was a partner in the local building firm of Dowsing and Davis. Many of the employees of the building firm over the years became members of the brigade. Romford also acquired two hospitals: one was the infirmary of the workhouse which kept growing and the other, whose funds were raised locally by the community, was the cottage hospital – the focus of a family doctor network in the town. Traditionally independent and competing doctors were willing to work together when accidents occurred or when children needed their help, often waiving their fees.

The gentle pace of life in Eastern Road, 1904. Today its length has been divided into two sections and the station end on the other side of the ring road is a very busy traffic artery.

Victoria Road, 1906. By the 1900s this had become significant as a shopping area, as several groups of traders ensured that most needs could be purchased close to the residents' front doors.

The Queen Victoria pub was one of two that served the neighbourhood; the other, the Royal Oak, was demolished for the ring road a few years ago. On the left of this 1910 photograph of Victoria Road is the Primitive Methodist church built in 1875, now used as a hall.

Como Street, 1906. It is a typical Victorian development of terraces, each group having a nameplate on the front elevation. In the 1870s the street was very short, extending only from North Street to the bridge over the Rom. Development came with the selling off for development of the Manor of Mawneys on the other side of the stream in 1883.

Junction Road, 1906. Here the left-hand side has only recently been developed, this top end having been a footpath between the lower section (built by 1854) and the main road until then. The right-hand side was to remain open for a couple of decades. The decorative detail and high Victorian and Edwardian design of the houses on the left make them worthy of preservation and restoration.

Prince's Road, with equally delightful Victorian housing, 1906. Manor Road, Prince's Road and King's Road were laid out in about 1886.

St Alban's Church at the junction of King's Road and Prince's Road was originally a mission under St Andrew's, serving this significant residential area. It opened in 1890. By the time of this view in 1905 development was extending to Heath Park Road in the north and Clydesdale Road to the south-east.

A quiet day in the Market Place, 1908. In the space of 100 years the growth of amenities changed Romford from being a very rural place to a more civilized town, although it was still a little rough at the edges. Note the street lamps and cobbles on the right and the public conveniences, drinking fountain and cattle trough on the left of the central roadway.

The entrance to the old cemetery, 1906. This opened in 1849 but was used only until 1871 when the new burial ground in Crow Lane took over. In 1953 the old cemetery minus its chapel, which was demolished, was redesigned as Coronation Gardens.

Laurie Square, 1920. Some idea of the peace that often reigned in this little oasis, shut off from the market proper by Laurie Hall, can be sensed in this view. Beyond the short length of Park End Road in the middle distance can be seen the fenced preserve of the Marshalls private estate. Four years later Marshalls was up for sale, and housing development followed.

Opposite. A rare view of Gresham Lodge, the house which originally stood on the site below the old cemetery. It has been replaced by pavement, roadway and the Town Hall forecourt.

The fire brigade have been called to a haystack fire — a frequent occurrence in the earlier years of the twentieth century when Romford was still surrounded by farmland. An early fire engine is recorded in 1787. In 1890 a volunteer brigade was formed by Samuel Davis, a local builder, and sponsored by the Romford Local Board, the then local authority.

Capt Davis' house, Mawney Road, 1907. As the builder of much of Victorian Romford, as well as being the fire chief, Samuel Davis was a well respected figure in the town and this is reflected in the fact that this postcard was printed of his house. The fire station at the bottom of Mawney Road was built next to the building yard and office of the firm of Dowsing and Davis, builders, and many of the firemen were recruited from the staff.

Motor fire engine and hose reel cart at the 1929 carnival. The new motor fire engine of 1922 was a Fiat with a 20.1 hp engine. Metcalf's coachbuilder's in the town made the fire engine body to fit the standard Fiat chassis according to the specification laid down by Capt Davis. The whole vehicle made up locally cost about half the price of one bought from elsewhere. Though small, the engine was adequate for the needs of Romford at the time. The pump was on the front of the Fiat and powered by its engine.

Entrance from Oldchurch Road to the Romford Union Workhouse, 1920. The old workhouse building still stands and is a unique survival of a 'Union' of 1839. As such it should be listed and preserved.

A doctor and nursing staff photographed outside the office of the Oldchurch Union Infirmary, 1900.

Task of
Work.

ROMFORD UNION.

Ordered by the *GUARDIANS of the ROMFORD UNION at a Meeting of the Board held this*
15th day of January, 1867.

That the MASTER of the WORKHOUSE of the ROMFORD UNION, do set
every Adult Person not suffering under any temporary or permanent Infirmity of
Body, being an occasional Poor Person, who shall be relieved in the said Workhouse, in return for the Food and Lodging afforded to such Person, to perform the
following TASK of WORK---that is to say :---

**MALES—To break two bushels of Stone to a size so as to
pass through a sieve provided for that purpose by the**
Guardians.

Provided that no such Person shall be detained against his will for the
performance of such Task of Work for any time exceeding Four hours from the
hour of Breakfast on the morning next after admission.

And provided also that such amount of Work shall not be required from
any Person to whose age, strength, and capacity, it shall appear not to be suited.

(Signed)   **W. H. CLIFTON,**
Clerk to the Guardians.

We, the POOR LAW BOARD, consent to, and approve of, the above Order of the Board of
Guardians of the ROMFORD UNION.

(Signed)

Dated this Thirtieth day of January, One
Thousand Eight Hundred and Sixty-seven.

GATHORNE HARDY,
President.

RALPH A. EARLE,
Secretary.

NOTICE.

Any such Person as above who shall, while in such Workhouse, *refuse* or *neglect* to
perform such Task of Work suited to the age, strength, and capacity of such Person,
will be deemed an *Idle* and *Disorderly* Person, and be liable to be *Imprisoned*
in the House of Correction, with Hard Labour, for *One Calendar Month.*

The prescribed task of work for those without other support entering the workhouse, dated 1867. This
was backbreaking work in exchange for a roof over the head and a basic meal. In the farming depressions,
every few years in the nineteenth century thousands of farmworkers found themselves in this
predicament. Others entered old age without any pension and unable to continue to earn a living. The
only option was to go into the workhouse, where food, shelter and medical care were available.

A rare glimpse of workhouse infirmary conditions, *c.* 1900. In the age before radio there were not many distractions for the patients to while away the time.

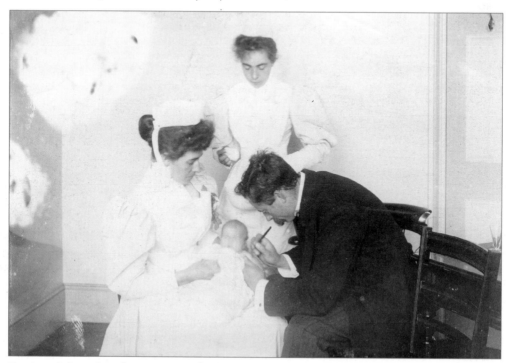

Treating a baby in the infirmary, 1900. The doctor and nurses put a great deal of loving care into helping their patients. Nevertheless, life for the ordinary working family at this time was very hard.

The Oldchurch Hospital developed from the workhouse infirmary and became larger and larger. The ward balconies are clearly visible. At the end of all main wards, they were meant to provide fresh air for the recuperating patients. This regime was sometimes pursued rather vigorously even in winter weather. The view southwards was for many years over open fields.

The Victoria Hospital, early twentieth century. The site had been given in 1887 by William Mashiter, and through public donations, money collected at carnivals and the efforts of local tradesmen and craftsmen this fine cottage hospital was built. It opened in 1888 and was so named to commemorate Victoria's Jubilee.

These gentlemen, connected with the workhouse/infirmary management, are talking in front of the institutional buildings, where someone has constructed a rockery garden.

A ventilator on the roof of the old workhouse – the buildings retain many interesting decorative and architectural features from the Victorian era.

The workhouse complex is a fascinating survival of Romford's past and should be retained. Modern uses could be found, for example as craft workshops or small business units, with a restored section housing a heritage display recording life in Romford 100 years ago.

At Romford station entrance, opposite Eastern Road, horse cabs await the arrival of a train, 1904. The view remained familiar for many years with the approach to the platforms accessed via the long walkways up the side of the original earth bank.

Underneath the Station Arch, 1920s. The old arch limited both the amount of rail traffic above and road traffic beneath. On Saturday 18 August 1930 four new 60 ft span girders were swung into position by travelling cranes to form the new bridge. This old brick arch of only 25 ft span was later demolished. The old railway bank had been extended northwards with a brick structure and pedestrian tunnels created inside, with a new lofty booking hall at street level. Fifty more trains a day were now laid on and services that formerly terminated at Ilford, Goodmayes or Chadwell Heath were extended.

Opposite. The platforms retained their country station appearance into the 1920s as there were still only two tracks running through. In January 1930 big changes occurred when a contract was entered into with McAlpine's for the widening of the section from Romford Junction to Romford railway factory. The project known as the Romford Railway Improvement Scheme, involved the complete rebuilding of Romford station.

These delightful villas in Western Road still stand to remind us of the great housing achievements of the 100 years up to 1914.

CHAPTER SIX

WE SERVE

Romford Library opened in the old Charity School building at the top end of the Market Place (The Pavement) in 1930. Essex County Council was persuaded to open this after much lobbying by the Rotary Club of Romford, which had been founded in 1922. The club was also instrumental in starting several other organisations in the area of social welfare. By the time Romford became a borough in 1937, choosing the motto 'Serve with Gladness' to complete its coat of arms, many of the services already operating in the town had been built up by the efforts of voluntary organisations and the self-help which was second nature to the people of the town.

An aerial view of the gas works, looking towards the town centre, early 1930s. Romford's first gas works were established in 1825 by George M. Bell in South Street, where a furnishing store now stands. The Romford Gas & Coke Co., formed in 1847, continued until 1949. The works at Nursery Walk were built in 1892 and by 1938 covered 25 acres. The buildings of Oldchurch Hospital, which were transferred to Essex County Council in 1930, can be seen beyond the gas works.

Patients at the Oldchurch Infirmary, 1920s. The more modern hospital was started in 1891 with what later became the administration block and A and B blocks. As medicine advanced and facilities improved the hospital became an important resource for the region.

The Nurses' Home, Oldchurch Infirmary, 1925. This was constructed along with C and D blocks in 1924. After Essex County Council took over in 1930, D block was extended and E block and the Nurses' Training School were completed in 1935 and 1936 respectively.

Church House, 1961. Partly dating from the fifteenth century, this building was originally a private home and later a priest's house for a short time, but for most of its history it was an inn. Latterly it was called the Cock and Bell, which closed down in 1908. Church House adds historical interest to a Market Place now stripped of its other old buildings. The Wykeham Hall behind was conceived as a social hall and meeting place for various activities and was at first known as the Romford Institute; it was built in 1909.

The new post office with postmen and customers outside, 1913. The smart motorcar may belong to Dr Alfred Wright, who was still living at 44 South Street, one of the two houses later demolished to make way for the shops beyond the post office. The post office in Romford moved frequently throughout the nineteenth century. At different times it was located at the Market Place, High Street and South Street (at the top end). The latter can be glimpsed in the top photograph on p. 127.

ROMFORD PARISH DIRECTORY.

The POST OFFICE is in High street, and Mr. Josiah Garnett is the *postmaster*. It is in the London Eastern Suburban District (E). Letters are despatched to London four times a day ; to Colchester, Suffolk, Norfolk, &c., at 8 night; and to Hornchurch, Dagenham, and surrounding villages, every morning. *Money Orders* are granted and paid from 9 morning till 6 evening, and here is a *Savings' Bank*. There are *sub-post offices* at Noak hill and Squirrel Heath.

Information on Romford postal services from White's 1863 directory, when the post office was in the High Street.

Opposite. Building the shop and office block by the post office, South Street, 1915. This site had originally been occupied by two houses with front gardens. Notice the number of men employed. The location of the new post office next door made this a desirable commercial site.

This Reliance company bus operated in Romford on the 366 route between the Green Man in Leytonstone and Brentwood from December 1928. The base was at Folly Lane, Chingford.

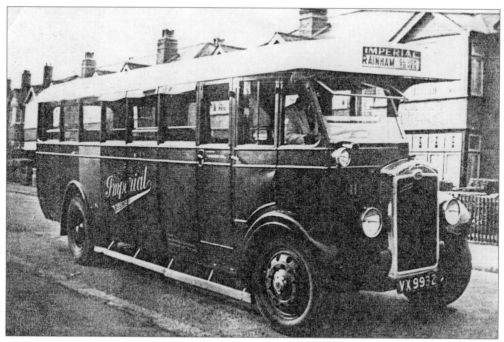

The Imperial buses, which ran from the local garage at 115–19 Marlborough Road, Romford, were started by Albert Edward Blane. At 27 years of age he was granted his earliest licences in April and May 1927. The green Imperials ran from Romford to South Hornchurch by way of Hornchurch Road and South End Road. The Romford District bus concern was already operating on this route.

A General ST type bus on route 66, one of the first routes to take advantage of the new Eastern Avenue bypass. According to the 1926 timetable the journey between Leytonstone and Gidea Park would take 54 minutes for a fare of 10d. The service ran in Romford via North Street, South Street and Victoria Road.

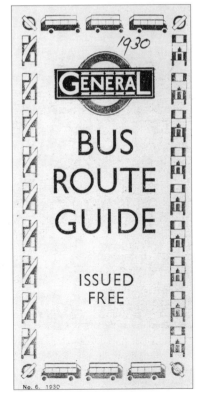

The General bus company route guide of 1930. By this time Romford had become quite a centre for bus services (routes 66, 86, 92, 123, 186, G1, G5, G40, 187 and 308 all operating here). This proliferation had been encouraged by the relatively poor train services and the fast population growth.

The 'City' company's typical six-wheeler bus was a familiar site in Romford Market Place on the Wood Green–Southend service, which was still operating until a decade ago, by Eastern National.

No.9L **CITY** 1936

TIME TABLE
of the
City Coach Company Ltd.
(Formerly New Empress Saloons Limited)
between
LONDON
LEIGHTON ROAD, KENTISH TOWN
(By Kentish Town Und. Station)
WOOD GREEN
AND
SOUTHEND ON SEA
TYLERS AVENUE, HIGH STREET

Cancels all previous issues.
Liable to revision without notice.

Telephones:
London   Southend-on-Sea
Gulliver 1176.   Marine 6479.

The 'City' company's London–Southend timetable of 1936 when the vehicles on this record-length bus service managed to keep to their schedules better than today's services. Buses operated through Romford every 15 minutes from 6.17 a.m. until 10.17 p.m.

The 'Westcliff' company also ran services between Southend and Romford – here is one of their vehicles by the Swan Inn, Romford Market, in the 1930s.

The 'Westcliff' Official Timetables booklet, 1936. Service 2a from Romford to Southend ran every hour from Romford via Hornchurch, Upminster and Laindon from 7.25 a.m. till 10.25 p.m.

A sudden outbreak of fire in a shop in Victoria Road, 1920s. A Romford Fire Brigade volunteer has climbed out on to the ledge above the shop awnings. A great amount of second-hand furniture is laid out on the pavement. The photograph was probably taken about midway up the road, from where the PDSA clinic and ring road are today.

CHAPTER SEVEN

A HIVE OF COMMERCE

*Looking down from the church tower to the National Provincial Bank (now the Co-op Bank) corner, over the west end
of the Market Place, 1950s. The town still retained the pattern of the amazing 1930s retail development with the
'Golden Mile' round the corner in South Street, the Quadrant Arcade running between the Market Place and South
Street, the Romford Arcade of 1930 facing Western Road (where the TSB now stands) and the Romford Shopping
Hall on the north side of the market. Many national stores had come to the town since the 1900s and this trend
gathered tremendous pace in the 1930s: Woolworths, Willerby's Tailor's, James Walker, Times Furnishing,
W.H. Smiths, Fifty Shilling Tailors, Dorothy Perkins, Marks & Spencer, Lilley and Skinner's footwear and J. Lyons'
teashop, all arrived to join older established multiples such as Sainsburys, Freeman, Hardy and Willis and Boots
chemist's. In the late 1960s and early 1970s the Romford Arcade interior was filled in and converted to ordinary large
shop units – the last traders in the arcade being Wells Music Store and a surgical goods shop. The new Liberty One
precinct opened, drawing the centre of shopping eastwards into its pedestrian malls and leaving South Street to play a
lesser role in the same way that earlier in the century the old High Street had had to yield the crown to South Street.*

Romford market in 1909 when most of the stalls were still full of items for farming use or produce for sale that had come from farms. Only a few stalls sold more general consumer goods. This changed later, as the farming contingent lessened.

Opposite. These impressively horned cattle are passing the Golden Lion almost casually. They were probably unloaded from a special train at the cattle dock station in Waterloo Road where there was an alighting ramp from the railway on its high bank above.

The Most Noted House for Drapery in Romford.

Near the old court house at the west end of the market was J.H. Sellers' drapers' business, seen here in
1905 when local shops held almost total sway in Romford.

The market crockery stall by The Lamb Inn, *c.* 1901. This is probably the stall of Mr Coles who stored his stock in a building in the yard behind the Lamb. He lost some of it in a fire there in 1911.

A close-up of Jarvis's shop at 104 Market Place in 1906 shows a recent addition to the family as well as a typical shop window display of this date.

Opposite. By the 1920s motorcars were beginning to appear in the Market Place when it was not in use. However there were not enough about to cause the parking problems and pollution experienced today. Many businesses had sprung up to cater for their needs. One was Romford Market Garage, seen on the left of the photograph on p. 101.

A market stall, with a glimpse behind of the Quadrant Arcade, 1951.

A view across the animal pens on a non-market day when Romford could sometimes seem unnaturally quiet, 1920s. Dozens of businesses line the south side of Market Place grouped on either side of the Bull Inn.

Opposite. Harry's shop at 104–6 Market Place, 1960s. This had become quite a Romford institution. It had been trading at this address for 50 years and for a short time before that in South Street. The original proprietor, Harry Sibley, came to Romford from Fulham in 1906.

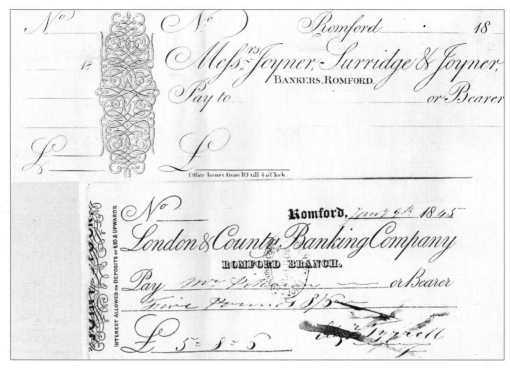

Two nineteenth-century cheques from Romford banks. The banks have played an important part in developing business in the town. In 1811 *Holden's Directory* lists two, Attersoll & Co. and Joyner & Co., and in 1823 Joyner, Surridge & Joyner were bankers in the High Street. However, in early 1826 the Romford Agricultural Bank was forced to close following a disastrous drain on its resources and later in 1844 came the failure of Johnson, Johnson and Mann.

Hill and Sons Bank, located on part of the site where Lloyds Bank now stands, was conveniently placed for the market. It is listed in 1899 as drawing funds from Hill & Sons of 66 Smithfield, London (another connection with the meat and cattle trade) and the better known Glyn, Mills, Currie & Co.

By the 1920s Lloyds Bank had supplanted Hill's at the corner.

The older Westminster Bank building in South Street which has been rebuilt with upper storeys on the same site. The original building with its vaults proved very difficult to demolish.

J. Cumberland's advertisement card, only slightly singed from being hung up in a smoky kitchen as suggested. James Cumberland was a poor boy of the Parish of Barking. In 1837 the parish bound him to John Marlin as an apprentice to learn the 'trade, business, art and mystery of a chimney sweeper' till he reached the age of 16. In 1851 we find Cumberland listed in the Census at Romford aged 24, along with Mary Ann aged 19 and a child, Mary Ann, of 13 months. He surfaces again as a chimney sweeper of High Street, Romford, in 1878. This bill states that he operated in Ray Square, which was a yard off the High Street, and may date from about 1860. Presumably his son and grandson carried on the business, as the firm appears as James Cumberland in directories of 1890 and 1910. By the latter date the address was 11 London Road. In 1912 the company is listed as J. Cumberland & Son. By 1937 it is listed as W.T. Cumberland who is probably the member of the family known as Wally; he appears in a photograph of the late 1920s astride a motor cycle with a sidecar, carrying a neat box containing sweeping brushes.

The first Romford Steam Laundry in Como Street. In the first six decades of this century, before the large-scale use of domestic washing-machines, there were half a dozen laundries in Romford.

Upper Bedfords/Parsonage Farm Dairies' shop, one of the many dairies in competition in the Romford area in the early part of the twentieth century, with a shop and depot in the town. This is believed to have been in the Victoria Road/Brentwood Road area. I would be interested to hear from anyone who could identify its position.

A view of some of the businesses in South Street, 1908.

Scruby's needlework and fancy goods shop at 7 South Street, in 1905. This sought to attract women's custom for craft materials and birthday and other presents. A relation of the proprietor had a shop in the High Street.

The top end of South Street, with the Fox & Hounds public house which was a meeting place for several Romford clubs, 1904. This whole block was taken down in the 1930s and the building line set back a considerable distance, thus widening this part of South Street.

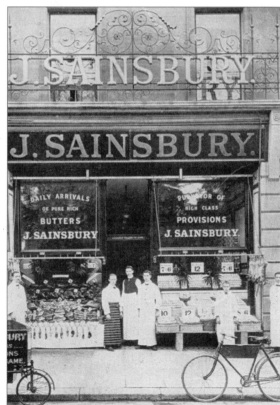

The original Sainsbury's branch in Romford at 30 South Street opened in this block of shops as soon as it was built, on previously open ground. It was to move further down the road to no. 46 in the mid-1920s.

The bottom end of Victoria Road was once dominated by Whitmore's Steam Flowermills, seen here in 1904. Horse and carts continually drew up to load and unload with the assistance of the overhead gantries. This mill, which replaced the old windmill, is now the site of a row of shops called Old Mill Parade.

Spiegel and Dook's shops in Victoria Road, 1929. Dook's was a short-lived venture, while Spiegel's was a well-established tailor's shop at no. 37.

Seen here during the First World War, Victoria Road's shopping developments were mainly in clusters which never completely superseded its original residential nature. Today there is still a significant housing element in its make-up.

A view of the shops at the corner of Park Lane on the edge of Hornchurch Parish towards Albert Road. This subsidiary shopping centre, with Sibthorp's shop on the right, a baker's on the left and further shops around the left corner in Brentwood Road, was very convenient for the large population nearby, saving them a trip into town.

Cheke & Co.'s auction and estate office in North Street was a familiar Romford landmark beyond the Golden Lion premises. This firm was one of several that participated in the twentieth-century housing boom in the area, but is now long gone.

South Street's 'Golden Mile' became busier and busier through the 1920s and '30s and large chain stores fought to locate there beside local names such as Thompson's, Wraight's, Hole's and Waller's (fishmonger's, draper's, ironmonger's and tailor's respectively).

The top end of South Street, showing the shops located in the old cottages on the left, 1908. Further along the tall building is the old post office, before it moved down the street. Note the shoeing smith's board on the right (Metcalfe).

In the late 1960s Romford still had its quaint corners. This view of Main Road shows the Victorian houses and cottages along the Town Hall frontage and the never-to-be-forgotten Tryst baker's and tearooms. Here you could still get a simple snack such as poached egg on toast for a very moderate charge into the 1970s. For the initiated there was the added delight of pushing through the bead curtain into the secluded tearoom at the rear – like travelling back in time to the 1920s.

INDEX